MW01196239

THE YEAR OF THE
HORSELESS CARRIAGE

1 8 O 1

BY GENEVIEVE FOSTER
ILLUSTRATED BY THE AUTHOR

BEAUTIFUL FEET BOOKS
SAN LUIS OBISPO, CALIFORNIA

Beautiful Feet Books
1306 Mill Street
San Luis Obispo, CA 93401
www.bfbooks.com
800.889.1978

Genevieve Foster
1893-1979

AMERICAN AUTHOR AND ILLUSTRATOR, GENEVIEVE FOSTER is credited with designing an entirely new genre of children's literature—the "horizontal history." Foster once noted, "history is drama . . . with men and nations as the actors. Why not present it with all the players who belong together on the stage at once rather than only one character on the stage at a time?" It was this novel idea that became the genesis for her "World" titles. *Abraham Lincoln's World* and *George Washington's World* were both awarded the prestigious Newbery Honor Medal and Foster went on to write five additional "World" titles including: *Captain John Smith, Columbus and Sons, William Penn* and *Augustus Caesar's World.* All of these are still popular today.

What made Foster's work so unique was her ability to select a central character and then to display all that was going on in the world around him not only on the geo-political scene, but also in science, philosophy, literature, music, and art. Her intuitive sense of what young readers want to know enhanced by her whimsical illustrations make history vibrant and immediate to her devoted readers.

The Year of the Horseless Carriage: 1801 presents the dawn of the 19th century with all its brilliant advancements in transportation, communication, and technology. While the world of technology is progressing rapidly, human rights and liberty are variously being trampled or rising. The megalomaniac Napoleon is proclaiming "liberty, equality, and fraternity" to a war-weary Europe, Jefferson is contemplating the largest land purchase in the history of the world, and Toussaint L'Ouverture is fighting for liberty in Haiti. Robert Livingston, Robert Fulton, Richard Trevithick, Beethoven, Lewis and Clark, Sacajawea, and Dolley Madison are all playing their parts. In this memorable retelling, youthful readers will come to appreciate why Foster was convinced that "history is drama."

Rea Berg—Publisher 2008

1801 1821

INTRODUCTION

IN 1801, WHEN THIS BOOK BEGINS, Napoleon Bonaparte was not only the ruler of France; he was also planning to conquer and rule over England, as well as the entire continent of Europe. In America he owned all the land from the Mississippi River to the Rocky Mountains. What he planned to do with it was of great concern to Thomas Jefferson, the new president of the United States.

In fact, in 1801, Napoleon was causing such a stir in both Europe and America that the invention of the "horseless carriage," the most significant event of that year, passed by almost unnoticed. It was not until Napoleon had been defeated by the kings and emperors of Europe, and was a prisoner on the island of Saint Helena, that the first public railroad was started in England and the locomotive began to take the place of the horse.

This is the story of those eventful twenty years—from 1801 to 1821. On the next page are the characters in the story, followed by a calendar of events.

Napoleon · Jefferson · Toussaint · Trevithick · Livingston · Fult

1801
RICHARD TREVITHICK invents the "horseless carriage."
THOMAS JEFFERSON becomes president of the United States.
NAPOLEON BONAPARTE is the ruler of France.
TOUSSAINT L'OUVERTURE becomes the ruler of Haiti.
BETHOVEN is writing a symphony dedicated to Napoleon.

1803
THOMAS JEFFERSON purchases Louisiana from Napoleon.
ROBERT FULTON tries out his first steamboat in Paris.
RICHARD TREVITHICK takes his steam carriage to London.

1804
RICHARD TREVITHICK runs the first locomotive on rails.
LEWIS and CLARK begin their expedition to the Pacific.
NAPOLEON declares himself emperor of France.
BEETHOVEN finishes his symphony—the *Eroica*.

1807
ROBERT FULTON runs his steamboat on the Hudson River.

1808
RICHARD TREVITHICK takes his locomotive to London.

Pompy the
ethoven · Lewis · Sacajawea · Clark · Madison · Dolley · Stephensons

1809 JAMES MADISON becomes president of the United States.

1812 PRESIDENT MADISON declares war against England.
NAPOLEON wages war against Russia.

1814 NAPOLEON abdicates in April and is taken to Elba.
GEORGE STEPHENSON makes his first locomotive in July.
THE WHITE HOUSE is burned by the British in August.
THE STAR-SPANGLED BANNER is written in September.

1815 NAPOLEON escapes from Elba on March 1,
is defeated at Waterloo on June 18,
and taken to Saint Helena on October 16.

1821 NAPOLEON dies.
GEORGE STEPHENSON builds the first public railway
in England.

CONTENTS

Part **III**

Part I _from_ 1801

RICHARD TREVITHICK

ROBERT FULTON

Richard Trevithick
SCOTLAND
Newcastle
THE TYNE
Stockton
Darlington
ENGLAND
WALES
Birmingham
PEN-Y-DARREN IRONWORKS
London
THE THAMES
Camborne
CORNWALL
THE ENGLISH CHANNEL

CHRISTMAS EVE : 1801

IT WAS THE AFTERNOON OF CHRISTMAS EVE, in the year 1801, that Richard Trevithick put the final touches on his steam carriage. He had been working on it for over a year, and though it was raining and the short winter's day was almost over, he could not wait for morning to try it out. He felt sure it would work. Some of his friends, however, had their doubts about it, as they watched him push it through the doorway of the blacksmith's shop onto the highway. There he lit the fire. Smoke and sparks poured from the tall chimney, steam hissed from the safety valve. It was ready to go! Seven or eight men jumped aboard and off they went up the hill to the Camborne harbor light and back again to the starting point. They could now boast of being the first ones ever to have ridden in a carriage hitched to a steam engine instead of a horse. They were proud to say that the inventor of the engine was a man of Cornwall, England, born and bred right there in Camborne.

They recalled how Dick, as a boy, had always had his own way of doing things. They remembered how one day in school he had thought up a quicker way for doing sums. And how the master had then punished him for not following the rule.

Richard Trevithick did not go far in school. He was too eager to see what was going on at the mine. His father was manager of several of the mines in Camborne, which, as you see on the map, is far down toward the tip of the island. Tin, copper, and lead had been mined there in the time of the ancient Phoenicians. So they were very old mines and very deep. Underground water collected in them and had to be continually pumped out—by hand—until a blacksmith named Newcomen invented a primitive steam engine to do the pumping.

In 1769, two years before Richard Trevithick was born, a Scotsman, James Watt, improved on Newcomen's engine so much that he became known as the inventor of the steam engine. Watt took out a patent and went into partnership with a man named Boulton. They built a factory to manufacture the engines, which they compared in power to so many horses. Thus the word *horsepower* came into use as a unit of measurement.

The year that Richard was six, the great James Watt came to Camborne to oversee the installing of two steam-engine pumps which Richard's father had purchased. Dick was fascinated by the pumps. The engine was huge, with great arms that went up and down. He spent hours watching and studying it after he quit school.

At first his father wanted him to stay in the office and not go wandering about among the tough workmen in the mines. But Dick was big for his age and well able to take care of himself. In fact, he grew so fast that by the time he was in his teens, he was being called a giant. One day in the counting house, a stranger, tired of hearing how strong this so-called giant was, challenged him to a wrestling match. Dick laughed, stood up, grabbed the man around the waist, turned him upside down, and pressed the soles of his boots against the ceiling. The dirty footprints were still there to be seen long after Richard Trevithick became famous as an engineer.

The first engine he designed was a new type for pumping, using what was then called "strong steam" (high-pressure steam). It was a much smaller engine than Watt's, in which the steam had no more pressure than in an ordinary teakettle. It was this small "strong steam" engine that had pulled that first load of passengers up to the Camborne light and back again on Christmas Eve.

Three days after Christmas, Trevithick and his cousin Vivian took the new steam carriage out for a second run. They had gone about a mile when the front wheels struck a gulley in the road, knocked the steering wheel out of Vivian's hands, and turned the carriage upside down in the ditch. They righted it, wheeled it into a shed, and went into a tavern nearby. They were enjoying a dinner of roast goose when a man rushed in: The shed was on fire! Nothing was left of shed or carriage.

Trevithick set to work at once on another steam carriage, which he and Vivian took by ship to London. There on a spring day in 1803 they drove it zigzagging down Oxford Street at the astounding speed of twelve miles an hour, terrifying horses and sending people scrambling from the path of the "devilish thing." It had ripped up sixteen feet of garden railing before they brought it to a stop. Trevithick was now convinced that the roads were too rough for his horseless carriage. It must have rails to run on. So he tore it apart, sold the carriage to one man, the engine to another, and went off to Wales to install one of his engines in an iron foundry.

And there at the foundry was a railroad! It had been built to carry products from the Pen-y'-Darren Ironworks to a canal ten miles away. Like all such early railroads it was intended for wagons drawn by horses.

"I can build an engine that will do the work better," Trevithick told the owner of the ironworks. The owner, ever ready to take a gamble, told him to go ahead.

"That's a crazy idea," said the owner of a rival ironworks, and bet 500 guineas that it couldn't be done.

"I'll take you up on that," said the owner of Pen-y'-

First locomotive
to run on
rails
+

1804

Darren. He bet 500 guineas that Trevithick's engine could haul ten tons of iron from the foundry to the canal.

On February 21, 1804, there was great excitement at both ironworks as the first locomotive ever to run on a railroad started out on this most important journey. The next day Trevithick wrote about it to a friend, saying:

"On our journey with the engine we carried 10 tons of iron, five waggons, and 70 men riding on them the whole journey. Its above 9 miles which we performed in 4 hours and 5 mints. The engine went nearly 5 miles per hour. The Gentleman that bet 500 guineas against it, rid the whole journey with us and is satisfied that he have lost the bet. The public till now called me a scheming fellow, but now their tone is much altered."

After this successful tryout, Trevithick was hopeful that his engine would be adopted, even though it would need heavier rails than those used by horses. But the ironworks owner said that it would not pay to rip up the railroad and lay a new one. However, he invited two engineers from the Navy Board in London to come to see the engine. Trevithick waited for them all summer long. They never came. So he tore the locomotive apart and used the engine for another purpose.

It is not surprising that members of the Navy Board would not leave London that summer to inspect some kind of steam carriage in Wales. Not *that* summer—when Napoleon Bonaparte was threatening to ship his army across the English Channel and invade England. Had it been a steamboat they had been asked to see, these navy men might have shown a little more interest.

"WHY CAN'T YOU DESIGN A STEAMBOAT? I am prepared to invest a considerable amount of money in a steamboat that can be used on the Hudson River."

This was Robert R. Livingston, whose home was on the Hudson River, speaking to Robert Fulton. The two Americans were in Paris. It was the spring of 1802. In December, Livingston had arrived as ambassador from the United States, having been appointed by President Thomas Jefferson.

from a portrait by
BENJAMIN WEST

Robert Fulton had been in Paris about five years and had some reputation as an inventor and also as an artist. He had started out in Philadelphia as a portrait painter. In 1786, when he was twenty-one, he had gone to London to study painting with Benjamin West, the famous Pennsylvania artist, who was royal painter to King George III.

Fulton had studied for about five years and was growing discouraged that it took so long for a painter to gain either fame or money, when, by chance, he met the duke of Bridgewater and was asked to paint his portrait.

The duke owned many coal mines and had just bought one of James Watt's pumping engines. He had also had a canal dug to carry coal from the mines. One day, as Fulton seemed interested, the duke took him to see the mines, the canal, and also to visit his marble quarries.

The marble, Fulton noticed, was being cut entirely by hand. Why, he thought, couldn't this slow, hard work be done by machine? He had an idea, sketched it out, and a few days later delighted the duke with an excellent design for a marble-cutting machine. Once he started thinking about mechanics, Fulton's mind was fairly seething with ideas. He designed a machine for dredging canals; he made a plan for lifting canal boats from one level to another without the use of locks. He then went to France hoping to sell these ideas. He also took with him what he considered by far his most important and worthwhile invention.

This was a design for a submarine, carrying a weapon so deadly that when it was placed under a large ship it would blow the ship to pieces. To this new weapon he gave the name of a deadly fish, calling it a *torpedo*.

Fulton felt sure that once the weapon was tested out, the mere fact that it existed would prevent war on the high seas and be a blessing to mankind, no matter who had it. Therefore, as soon as he got to Paris, he wrote directly to Napoleon, assuring him that his "glory would be as durable as time" if he would but use this weapon to promote world peace. Also, since the British navy was larger and stronger than that of France, Fulton offered to build a submarine at his own expense if Napoleon would agree to pay him a certain sum for each British warship over forty guns sunk by his torpedoes.

An American poet, with whom Fulton went to live in Paris, remembered that in 1776 a submarine called *The Turtle* had been tried out in New York harbor by General Washington. Fulton said his design was such an improvement over *The Turtle* as to be practically original.

Needing money to build his submarine, Fulton turned back to painting. With a partner he built a huge circular building on one of the boulevards. Around the inside he painted an imaginary scene of "The Burning of Moscow" and charged admission to see the panorama. It was so popular that it made more money than he needed.

In the summer of 1800, Fulton's newly built submarine, called *The Nautilus,* was tested out in the Seine. Paris crowds gathered along the banks to watch, cheered as the American and his helper submerged, remained under water twenty minutes, and reappeared, unharmed.

The torpedo itself was tried out before a number of navy officers appointed by Napoleon. This trial took place in the harbor of Brest where an old sloop was anchored. The submarine submerged, placed the bomb containing twenty pounds of gunpowder under the ship's hull, and got away safely while the ancient sloop was blown to bits.

The delighted inventor was now ready for the supreme test of blowing up two British brigs that were blockading a French harbor. Fulton sailed *The Nautilus* as near to them as he dared, then submerged. Down in the dark, the four men, cranking the paddle wheel by hand, moved ahead so slowly that before they reached them, the brigs had hoisted their sails and were gone! Gone, too, was any interest Napoleon may have had in Fulton's submarine.

Very soon, however, the disappointed inventor had an invitation from the British government to bring his submarine to England. There the navy insisted that their own sailors make the test. So it failed again, and Fulton returned to France, disappointed that it took so long for an inventor to gain either money or fame. It was then by chance that he met Robert R. Livingston and was glad to accept the ambassador's proposal to design a steamboat to be used on the Hudson River.

There was nothing new about trying to design a steamboat. Robert Fulton was well aware of that. Dozens of people had tried and failed, for one reason or another, to keep their boats running. While he was still in Philadelphia, a steamboat built by John Fitch had run all one summer on the Delaware River up to Trenton and back, and then disappeared.

The very year that Fulton and Livingston met in Paris, a steamboat was built in Scotland by an inventor named William Symington. It was tried out in a canal and ran well, but the canal owners feared that its paddle wheels might wash away the banks and forbade its use.

Robert Fulton began his work by carefully studying

all the steamboats that had been made so far. He added changes and improvements for his final design. He then had the engine built by one French manufacturer, had the boat built by another. And by the summer of 1803 it was ready to be tried out in the Seine.

The test was reported in a Paris journal, which said: "On August 9th a trial was made of a new invention—a boat of strange appearance, with wheels like a cart, those wheels being provided with paddles and moved by a fire engine. The author of this brilliant invention is Mr. Fulton, an American and celebrated engineer."

By this time Livingston had written the legislature in Albany, New York, and received from them the exclusive right to run a steamboat on the Hudson River.

The engine for the Hudson River steamboat was ordered by Robert Fulton from Boulton and Watt. He would have to wait three years for it to be delivered.

In the meantime, he tried again to interest the English government in his submarine, and failed again. It was over a hundred years too soon for the world to accept the submarine; not until 1914 were submarines successfully used by the Germans in the First World War.

Part II from 1803

NAPOLEON : CONQUEROR

THOMAS JEFFERSON

TOUSSAINT L'OUVERTURE

LEWIS AND CLARK

NAPOLEON : EMPEROR

BEETHOVEN

MOSCOW⊙

RUS

AUSTRIA

LONDON⊙

HOLLAND

Boulogne
Waterloo

PARIS⊙

FRANCE

CORSICA

ELBA

SPAIN

0   10

England and her
allies against
Napoleon

Amount of Europe under
Napoleon's control
by 1812

Napoleon Bonaparte

NAPOLEON WAS NOT IN PARIS in the summer of 1803, when Robert Fulton tested out his steamboat. Napoleon was in the harbor of Boulogne, preparing to conquer England by shipping his troops across the English Channel. From where he stood he could look across that "ditch," as he scornfully called the Channel, and see the shores of England in the distance. One day he would be there as the conqueror, riding into London at the head of his victorious troops. He was so sure of this that he had already had a gold medal made for the occasion, bearing the words: STRUCK IN LONDON, 1804.

Who was this man—Napoleon Bonaparte? What had he done that could make him so sure of himself?

First of all, though Napoleon was the ruler of France, he was not a Frenchman. He was of Italian parentage, born on the island of Corsica. In 1779, when he was ten, his family had moved to France and put him into a French school, where he had been miserable, ridiculed for his Italian accent and his peculiar name. At fifteen, being very bright, he had been promoted to a military school in Paris, where he was the shortest boy in his class. They called him "the little Corsican."

His career as a soldier had begun during the French Revolution, when the people of France rebelled against the king, seized the government, and turned it into a republic. The year that the king, Louis XVI, was beheaded on the guillotine, Napoleon Bonaparte was a captain in the Republican army. Two years later, he was a general, fighting to defend the new Republic from its enemies both within and without. Within France were many royalists, still loyal to the king and fighting to overthrow the Republic and restore the kingdom. Outside France were all the kings of Europe, fighting to protect themselves from the dangers of the revolution.

The two most powerful enemies of the French Republic were Austria and England. Napoleon first fought against Austria, and in a few lightning battles he won all of Austria's land in northern Italy. Next he tried to capture Egypt and so block England's route to India (which then belonged to England). He had gone inland as far as the pyramids when he heard that the English navy, under Admiral Nelson, had completely destroyed the ships that had brought the French army to Egypt. Deserting his soldiers, Napoleon slipped away alone in a small boat headed for France. As soon as he landed, he sent word ahead to Paris that Egypt had been conquered, so that when he, himself, arrived in Paris he would be welcomed as a hero.

Very soon the five unpopular men directing the government were overthrown and the hero Napoleon was elected First Consul, head of the French Republic. It was then 1799. Although France was still called a republic, it was again under the rule of one man, not a king this time, but a military dictator—Napoleon Bonaparte.

In 1800, he was off again to Italy, where he defeated an Austrian army for a second time. Next, after a brief truce, he prepared to resume his battle against England. Someone said it was like an elephant trying to fight a whale. Napoleon had the greatest army in Europe, but England had the greatest navy on the seas.

This cartoon (*right*) shows the world as a plum pudding on which the prime minister of England and Napoleon are about to dine, the one cutting off a large slice of the ocean, while the other slices off Europe.

As Napoleon had no hope of defeating England at sea, he conceived the fantastic plan of shipping his army across the English Channel on mammoth flatboats. To prevent the English navy from blocking the way, he planned to send the French fleet off to the West Indies and lure Admiral Nelson and the English fleet into chasing after them. Then, before Nelson had time to return from that wild-goose chase, he, Napoleon, would have his army across the Channel and be riding into London!

So in the spring of 1803, Napoleon was in Boulogne

to oversee this gigantic undertaking. Twelve hundred
boats had to be built to ship an army of 150,000 soldiers
to England. This took an immense amount of money. To
get what he needed Napoleon had what he thought was a
brilliant idea: He would sell the French colony of Louisiana to the United States! As quick to act as he was to
think, Napoleon wrote at once to his foreign minister in
Paris to offer Louisiana to the United States ambassador
for 60 million francs. So while that ambassador, Mr. Livingston, was waiting to see Robert Fulton's steamboat
tried out on the Seine, he was astounded and delighted
at being offered all of Louisiana—and for a mere 60
million francs—15 million dollars—which would
amount to only about two and a half cents an acre!

THOMAS JEFFERSON, who was to purchase Louisiana from Napoleon, had become president of the United States in 1801. He was the first president to take the oath of office in the new Capitol building, which some

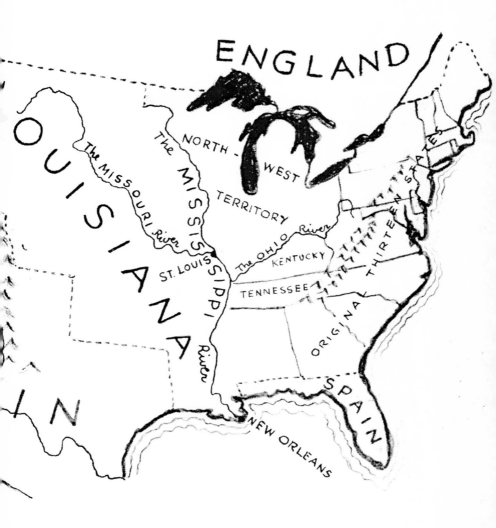

people referred to as a "palace in the backwoods."

Washington, D.C., was then just a scraggly village of a few hundred inhabitants. Many members of Congress who came from cities along the Atlantic Coast felt that

33

the site selected for the nation's capital city was much too far west.

Jefferson did not agree with them. His own home, Monticello, was still farther west. From there to Washington was four days' journey on horseback, if the roads (which were hardly more than trails) had not been washed out by rain or blocked by fallen trees.

It was true that all the states, of which there were then sixteen, were east of the Appalachian Mountains, except the two newest, Kentucky and Tennessee, which reached to the Mississippi River. That was as far as the United States went. And as far as it ever would or should go, many people believed.

Again Jefferson disagreed with them about the West. He believed that when the population reached ten persons to the square mile, "it would spill over the river and push west in great numbers in search of vacant country." Farmers were already living west of the Appalachians, and sending their produce to market down the Mississippi River. Flour, tobacco, lard, feathers, butter, cheese, apples, and cider were floated down on flatboats to be sold at once or stored for export in New Orleans.

New Orleans belonged to Spain. French explorers had discovered and named all of the river valley "Louisiana" for Louis XIV, the king of France. The next king, Louis XV, had ceded it to Spain. So long as Spain held New Orleans, Jefferson felt reasonably certain that Americans would be allowed to use that port. But soon after he took office, he was alarmed to hear that Napoleon had forced Spain to give all of Louisiana back to France! This was a serious problem. Who could possibly imagine, he thought, what that "determined villain" had in mind!

Jefferson had then appointed as ambassador to France a distinguished gentleman whom he had known for many years, Robert R. Livingston. In 1776, Mr. Livingston had been on the committee appointed to draw up the Declaration of Independence, which Jefferson had later written. Later, as judge, or chancellor, of New York, Livingston had administered the oath of office to George Washington.

Jefferson told Livingston to try to purchase New Orleans and some of the nearby land east of that city as soon as he arrived in Paris. The ambassador left for France in late fall. As it took over a month to cross the

Atlantic, he did not reach Paris until December, 1801.

Later, Jefferson, growing more and more worried about New Orleans, sent James Monroe to France to see what was happening. In April, 1803, when Monroe arrived in Paris, he was amazed to learn that Livingston had been given the chance to buy not merely New Orleans from Napoleon, but the entire Louisiana Territory! The agreement, or treaty, was promptly signed by the two Americans and sent on for Jefferson's signature to make it official.

And so, by merely signing his name, Thomas Jefferson more than doubled the size of the United States. Over a million square miles were added, reaching from the Mississippi River to the Rocky Mountains—over 600 million acres and for only two and a half cents an acre!

The Louisiana Purchase was the greatest event in the eight years that Jefferson was president. It is also considered one of the three major events in American history. The other two are the Declaration of Independence, which made the United States the first independent nation in the Western world, and the Emancipation Proclamation, which gave the slaves their freedom.

Toussaint L'Ouverture

THE CHANCES ARE THAT NAPOLEON would
never have sold Louisiana to the United States if he had
not first lost the island of Haiti. Napoleon had planned

to make this lovely Caribbean island the heart of a great overseas empire, which would have included Louisiana.

Although only half of the island belonged to France—the other half to Spain—it was still her most valuable colony. Its moist green hillsides were covered with coffee orchards and rich fields of cotton and sugarcane.

Unfortunately, the people living on this lovely island were divided by the color of their skins into three unfriendly groups: black, white, and colored. There were about five hundred thousand black slaves who did all the work, and about forty thousand white planters who lived in luxury. And in between—thirty thousand free "colored" people, the result of the union of black and white, who were looked down upon by the whites as they in turn looked down upon the blacks.

News of the French Revolution was the spark that turned the smoldering hatred of Haiti's oppressed population into actual rebellion. As soon as the colored people heard that the revolution stood for "liberty and equality," they sent a delegate to France to ask for civil rights equal to those of the white planters. When the delegate returned successful, he and a friend were seized by the white planters and beheaded. Their bloody heads, stuck on poles, were carried through the streets of Le Cap, the main city of Haiti.

One of three black men who saw the bloody procession that day was an elderly coachman named Toussaint, a very small, thin man in an elegant blue and red uniform, driving his master's wife into town from a nearby plantation. Unlike most slaves, he had been kindly treated by his master and given a very fine education, including French and Roman history, philosophy, geography, and mathematics. '

Another observer that day was a burly, broad-chested man who had come from Africa on a slave ship and had no education at all. His name was Dessalines.

A third, the slave of an innkeeper, was a waiter in a long white apron, standing in the tavern doorway as the procession passed. His name was Christophe.

All three were to take part in Haiti's fight for freedom. This fight began in August, 1791, when over a hundred thousand slaves rose in revolt against their owners. In two weeks six hundred coffee plantations were destroyed, two hundred sugar refineries were burned to the ground. More than one hundred owners were dragged out and slaughtered.

Toussaint saw his master and the family safely off for the United States before he joined the rebellion. Soon he became the leader. By that time soldiers had arrived from France to crush the rebellion. The French general was amazed at the speed and skill with which Toussaint moved his men in and out of the mountains.

"He seems able to find an opening wherever he needs one," exclaimed the Frenchman. *Ouverture* is the French word for "opening," so from then on Toussaint was known as Toussaint L'Ouverture.

Very soon the Spanish, happy to see the French in trouble, sent troops in from Santo Domingo to try to recapture the rest of the island, which had originally belonged to Spain. Toussaint joined forces with the Spanish, until word came from France that what he was fighting for—freedom of the slaves—had been granted by the new Republic.

Turning about at once, he offered his grateful services to the French Republic, drove the Spanish out of Haiti, and then captured Santo Domingo. In 1801, just ten years after the rebellion began, Toussaint L'Ouverture was ruler of the entire island, Santo Domingo as well as Haiti.

He had a constitution drawn up and sent to Paris for the approval of Napoleon Bonaparte, who had by then become the ruler of France.

Napoleon was furious. He had no use for that insolent black man, whom some people were actually calling the "Bonaparte of Haiti"! Napoleon's answer to him was to send to Haiti an army of 40,000 soldiers on eighty-six warships, under the command of his brother-in-law, Le Clerc. He gave Le Clerc just two months to defeat the old black man and restore slavery to the island.

In four months Le Clerc lost seventeen thousand men fighting against Toussaint and had to call for an armistice. Hardly had Toussaint entered the treaty room than he was seized, bound as a prisoner, and hustled aboard a ship sailing for France.

There, Napoleon had him locked up in a mountain fortress, where the old hero, who was then sixty years of age, died of cold and starvation.

Meanwhile, back in Haiti, the blacks, infuriated by this treachery, renewed their struggle for freedom under the command of Dessalines.

During their first summer in the tropics, thousands of French soldiers sickened and died of yellow fever. By fall, Le Clerc, too, was dead.

Napoleon then made the quick decision to save face— forget about Haiti, give up the whole idea of a colonial empire, and sell Louisiana to the United States.

Dessalines, who had won the final fight for freedom, was made governor for life. He started his rule with a savage massacre of his white subjects. Then in 1804, he proclaimed himself emperor, but proved to be such a tyrant that two years later he was murdered.

In 1810, after fighting for power, Christophe declared himself king. Ten years later his cruelty caused a rebellion, and he shot himself with a silver bullet.

Though the lives of the three black leaders ended in tragedy, the freedom they won for the island was never lost. They made Haiti the second independent nation in the Western Hemisphere, as well as the oldest black republic in the modern world.

SIX MONTHS BEFORE THOMAS JEFFERSON purchased Louisiana, he had spoken to Congress about exploring the land west of the Mississippi River and Congress had given him $2,500 to use for that purpose. Jefferson had then chosen Captain Meriwether Lewis to head the exploration. Jefferson had known young Lewis since he was a small boy and felt that he could not have made a better choice.

As for Captain Lewis, the idea suited him exactly. As long as he could remember he had dreamed of finding the source of the Missouri River. He had been stationed at Fort Detroit when, in the spring of 1801, he had had a request from the new president to come to Washington to be his secretary. In the two years he had lived and worked with Jefferson in the President's House, they had spent many hours making plans for the expedition.

One project had to do with a corner of unexplored land in the far northwest. Ten years before, an American had sailed up the Pacific coast and into the mouth of a large river, which he had named the Columbia. The British were eager to make that river basin part of Can-

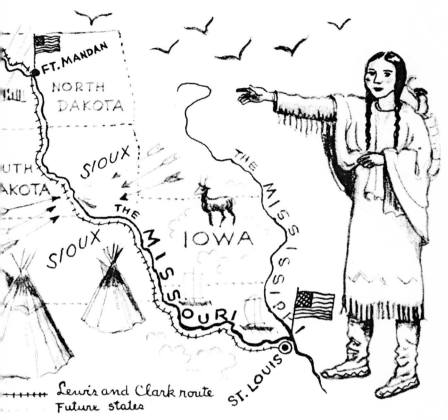

Lewis and Clark route
Future states

ada, and Jefferson knew that they were already searching for the source of the river. If the Americans could find it first and follow the Columbia to the Pacific Ocean, all land along the river would belong to the United States.

The entire expedition, Jefferson realized, would be dangerous and should have two leaders, so that if something happened to one, the other could carry on. Lewis chose William Clark, a boyhood friend, who was also an officer in the army. They had always gotten along well together, although they were very different. Lewis was a scientist, quiet, tall, and rather dignified.

William Clark was full of energy and bounce, with bright red hair, a kind, friendly manner, and a very warm heart. He brought with him his servant York, an equally friendly man, who was to enjoy the amazement he caused the Indians who had never seen a black man before.

By November, 1803, Lewis and Clark had reached the Illinois side of the Mississippi, across from Saint Louis. There they spent the winter preparing for their great adventure, buying food supplies, medicines, scientific instruments, and articles for trading with the Indians. They enlisted twenty-eight frontiersmen into an army to go with them, all supplied with guns and ammunition. Lewis had bought a river barge with a high square sail, which took twenty men to row, and by spring the men had built two smaller boats, with oars and sails.

On May 14, 1804, with the firing of a single shot, the expedition started from Saint Louis up the Missouri River, the stars and stripes flying from the mast of the largest ship. Even with twenty men at the oars, it was tough, slow rowing upstream against the strong current.

Summer came soon, and with it the blazing sun and scorching heat of the prairies. They had passed safely through the land of the warlike Sioux before they felt the first chills of autumn and saw the first wild geese flying south. Flurries of snow came as they reached the village of the Mandans, a peaceful tribe of Indians, whose chief gave them a cordial welcome. Near the chief's lodge the explorers built a log fort in which to spend the winter.

The Indians said that the Missouri began far to the sunset in the "Shining Mountains." To cross the mountains they would need horses. The Shoshoni who lived in the mountains had horses, but the Shoshonis never came down to the plains unless they were starving and on the hunt for buffalo.

One day before Christmas, a French Canadian fur trader named Charbonneau came to the fort to ask for the job of guide and interpreter. His wife, he said, was a Shoshoni Indian. She had been captured by another tribe, and he had bought her from them. Her name was Sacajawea.

In February, Sacajawea had a baby boy. Clark said that

47

the French name she gave him was too hard to say. So he called him Pompy, the Indian word for "first born." Sacajawea had made a cradle for him, and very soon the bright-eyed baby boy was riding about on her back.

By the time the bitter-cold winter was over, the men had hollowed out six large tree trunks into canoes. From there on, the river would be too shallow for the big boat, so it was sent back to Saint Louis loaded with furs. One of the smaller boats now became the flagship. It carried the medicines, the scientific instruments, and the records. Usually Sacajawea sat in front with Pompy on her back and Lewis's dog sitting beside her.

One day in May, when Lewis and Clark had both gone ashore to look about, a raging storm suddenly came up. The boat almost capsized. Lewis was about to plunge into the river to rescue the records and instruments, when they saw Sacajawea, with Pompy on her back, collecting all the valuables washed overboard.

Day by day, as they paddled on, the river grew narrower and the mountains on either side rose higher and higher. Late in July, they came to a place where three rivers met to form the Missouri. Sacajawea pointed to the western branch.

"Near where that river begins," she said, "live my people, the Shoshoni."

Lewis decided that he and three men should go ahead on foot to the land of the Shoshoni. Sacajawea told him, as a sign of peace, to spread a blanket wide and wave it over his head three times.

The river soon became a rushing mountain stream as the men walked beside it, then a tiny brook which they could step across, ending in a bubbling spring. So here it was! The source of the mighty Missouri! And just beyond the next mountain they came to a brook flowing *west* instead of *east,* and therefore knew that they had crossed the Continental Divide. They had gone beyond the Louisiana Territory—into unclaimed land.

Suddenly, as they climbed over the edge of a ravine, they found themselves face to face with three Indian women. Instead of killing them, as the women expected, Lewis marked their faces with red paint, as Sacajawea had told him to do, and gave them beads and mirrors.

Soon fifty or sixty warriors came galloping up on their horses. The chief, seeing the red paint on the women's faces, jumped from his horse and rubbed his cheek against that of Lewis, who then persuaded the Indian to go back with him to meet the other white men coming up the river.

As soon as Sacajawea and the young chief saw each other, they ran into each other's arms in almost unbelievable joy. The chief was Sacajawea's brother!

She assured him that he could trust the white men, in spite of their guns. They only wanted horses, in order to cross the Shining Mountains.

Leaving their boats hidden on an island, the explorers now began the hardest part of their journey, crossing the Rocky Mountains on horseback. Day after day the cliffs grew steeper and more treacherous. And there was nothing ahead but row after row of snow-covered peaks—nothing to do but struggle on through hail and blinding sleet—and gnawing hunger when the food gave out.

Finally, far below, through an opening in the clouds, they saw a green valley. Arriving there, they found the Nez Percé Indians, whose chief said that their river, which was full of salmon, ran into a larger river, which ran into a "Bitter Shoreless Lake." Leaving the horses with the Nez Percé, the travelers started down the river in five new dugout canoes. Going with the current, they sped along and, by mid-October, entered the Columbia. All day, the seventh of November, they paddled through a heavy fog, when suddenly the fog lifted, and there before them were the shining waves of the Pacific Ocean. So now all the land through which they had come belonged to the United States! Lewis and Clark carved their names on trees near the bay with the words:

BY LAND FROM THE UNITED STATES IN 1804 AND 1805

HERE IS NAPOLEON BONAPARTE, the world's most famous man on the greatest day of his life, December 2, 1804, when he became the emperor of France. The coronation took place in the cathedral of Notre Dame. The pope had made a special journey from Rome to perform the ceremony. But when the moment came for Napoleon to kneel before the Holy Father to be crowned, he seized the crown from the pope's hand and crowned himself with a golden laurel wreath, like that worn by emperors of ancient Rome. From then on, like all kings and emperors, he would be called by his first name only. Here the new, self-crowned Emperor Napoleon is crowning his wife—the Empress Josephine.

By early spring Napoleon was back again at Boulogne carrying on his plans for invading England, which so far were going along well. The French fleet had sailed for the West Indies, and Admiral Nelson and the English

DECEMBER 2

1804

from a huge painting by DA

Napoleon I

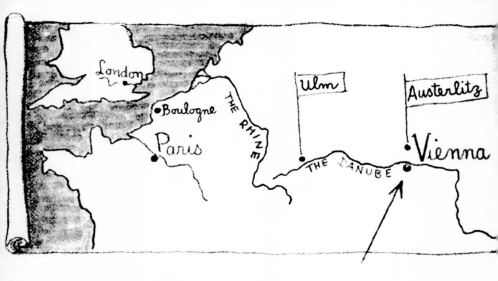

fleet were chasing after them, as Napoleon had hoped they would, leaving the English Channel unprotected. Napoleon was about ready to ship his troops across to conquer England, when news came making that impossible: England had drawn both Austria and Russia into an alliance against him. This meant that all those troops he had been expecting to ship to England would have to be used in eastern Europe against the armies of Austria and Russia!

Pacing back and forth in the country house he used for headquarters, Napoleon dictated to an officer the exact line of march the soldiers were to take on the way to Austria. Without referring to any map, he was able to calculate the exact date of their arrival at every town along the way. Keeping the speed of fifteen miles a day, by the end of September, Napoleon had crossed the Rhine with 190,000 men. Three weeks later he was at the city of Ulm. There he surprised and defeated an Austrian general who had had no idea that Napoleon could possibly move his army so fast.

Just two days after this victory, a messenger brought Napoleon news of a shocking defeat.

The French fleet, after returning from the West Indies, had been destroyed by the English fleet under Admiral Nelson. A dreadful sea battle had taken place on October 21, off Cape Trafalgar on the coast of Spain. With this defeat died any lingering hope Napoleon may still have had of invading England. Doubling his speed he rushed on toward Vienna, Austria's capital city.

NAPOLEON'S MOST FAMOUS BATTLE came on December 2, 1805, near the small village of Austerlitz, not far from Vienna. It is sometimes called the battle of the three emperors, for the other two were also there, the Austrian emperor, Francis I, and the Russian emperor, Alexander I.

Their armies, under the command of a Russian general, were separated from the French army by a long, narrow plateau, shaped like a whale. At one end of the plateau was a bridge crossing a small river. The French were stationed near one end of the bridge. They also occupied a hill at the opposite end of the plateau.

Napoleon's scheme was to tempt the Russian commander into attacking the French troops at both places at the same time. As soon as that happened a third group of French troops was to rush across the center of the pla-

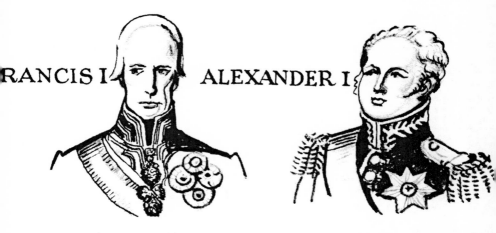

FRANCIS I   ALEXANDER I

teau, cut the enemy line in two, and attack both sections from the rear.

One night, as Napoleon was eating a supper of potatoes and onions in a peasant's hut, he got word that the enemy troops were moving in both directions.

"Aha!" he shouted, rubbing his greasy hands together. "I've got them. They're walking into my trap!"

Before the sun had set the next day, Napoleon was galloping along the plateau, calling out to the soldiers that the battle had been won. Later, by candlelight, he wrote a letter to Josephine, saying:

"I have beaten the Russian and Austrian armies commanded by the two emperors. I am rather tired . . . I hope to sleep for two or three hours. . . ."

The next day, Napoleon was at the palace of Schönbrunn in Vienna, there to dictate a treaty of peace.

LUDWIG VAN BEETHOVEN LIVED IN VIENNA, only a half hour's ride by carriage from the palace of Schönbrunn, where Napoleon was dictating the treaty of peace. This fact was of no interest whatever to Napoleon, who had never heard of the pianist and composer and cared nothing about music.

Beethoven, on the other hand, had followed Napoleon Bonaparte's career with great interest and with great admiration until a year before, when he had been bitterly disappointed. Up to the time that Napoleon declared himself emperor, he had been Beethoven's hero.

Beethoven had first heard of the "little Corsican" as a lieutenant in the French Revolution, fighting for the rights of the common people. Soon he had seen Bonaparte proving by his own success that in the Republic a man who had neither royal nor noble blood could still become a person of importance. As First Consul, Bonaparte had then established a new Code of Laws to safe-guard the rights of the common people of France. And then this hero-statesman had proclaimed that what he had done for France, he would do for Europe. He would free all the people of Europe from oppression by kings and emperors and unite them in one great republic where "liberty, equality, and fraternity" would forever prevail!

And indeed, in 1796, after Bonaparte had won his first victory over the Austrian army in Italy, he had es-tablished republics both in Genoa and Milan. This espe-cially impressed Beethoven, who knew well how people suffered under the arrogant rule of the Austrian emperor.

It was then that he decided to write a symphony dedi-cated to his hero. Actually the suggestion was made by one of Bonaparte's generals who had been stationed in Vienna. He was a splendid young Frenchman named Bernadotte (who later became the king of Sweden).

Soon after Bernadotte's visit, Beethoven began to sketch out what was to become known as the *Eroica* Sym-phony, or, according to its title in Italian,

SINFONIA EROICA.

Of the nine symphonies which Beethoven composed, the *Eroica* is the third.

The first one of the nine, the C Major, was introduced in 1800 and played by the composer himself in a public concert. The announcement read:

Today, Wednesday, April 2, 1800,
Herr Ludwig van Beethoven
will have the honor to give a
grand concert for his benefit
at the Royal Imperial Court Theater.
Tickets for boxes and stalls
are to be had of Herr van Beethoven,
at his lodgings in the
Tiefen Graben No. 241, third story,
and of the box keeper. Prices of admission are as usual.
The beginning is at half past six.

By the end of that year, 1800, the Austrian army had been defeated by Napoleon for the second time. Wounded soldiers were pouring into Vienna, and funds were needed for their relief. One way of raising money

was by public concerts. At one of these concerts Franz Joseph Haydn conducted his oratorio, *The Creation.* At another, both Haydn and Beethoven took part. Haydn was then sixty-eight; for a short time he had been Beethoven's teacher. Although Beethoven was only thirty, he was already growing deaf. Even the sound of his own playing was hard for him to hear. Fortunately the deafness did not interfere with his composing. As he wrote the notes on the staff, he could hear the sound of their music in his mind.

Grande
Simphonie
2 Violons, Viole
Violoncelle et Basse
2 Flutes, 2 Oboes, 2 Cors
2 Bassons, 2 Clarinettes
2 Trompettes et Timbales
par
Louis van Beethoven

C Major, first played April 2, 1800

In the *Eroica,* Beethoven was hoping to express those noble qualities of mind and heart which make a man worthy to be called a hero—qualities which he truly believed Napoleon Bonaparte possessed.

By the spring of 1804, Beethoven had his symphony completed. A copy of the original score had been made and was ready to be sent to Paris. A friend who came by saw the score lying on the table with the name of Bonaparte on the title page.

He then gave Beethoven the latest news from Paris, saying that Napoleon Bonaparte had declared himself emperor—that the coronation would take place later that year, probably in December. That before this declaration, Napoleon had ordered a nobleman put to death, accused of plotting to assassinate him. Even though the nobleman had been proved innocent, Bonaparte had him brought before the firing squad and shot!

At this shocking news, Beethoven sprang to his feet, flew into a terrible rage, and cried out:

"So he too is nothing but an ordinary man! Now he too will trample on the rights of people. He too will become a tyrant!"

Seizing the symphony, he ripped off the title page, tore it to pieces, and threw it on the floor. Later, from another copy of the title page, Beethoven erased the name Bonaparte in such fury that he wore a hole in the paper.

The *Eroica,* though no longer dedicated to Napoleon, was performed for the first time on April 7, 1805, with Beethoven conducting. And it was always to remain his own favorite of the nine symphonies.

$\mathcal{P}art$ **III** $^{from}_{1807}$

RICHARD TREVITHICK
ROBERT FULTON
JAMES MADISON
NAPOLEON: DEFEATED
GEORGE STEPHENSON

LONDON : 1808

from a drawing by Thomas Rowlandson made the next year

Catch me who can

THIS IS THE THIRD AND LAST LOCOMOTIVE built by Richard Trevithick. In the spring of 1808, he took it to London. There, on a vacant lot, he built a circular track, enclosed it with a high fence, and charged one shilling admission to the arena.

He called the engine the *Catch Me Who Can* and advertised that he would race it for twenty-four hours against the fastest horse in the kingdom. He waited for days. But nobody brought a horse to race against his engine, and so few people paid admission to see it or ride in the carriage that the sum he took in did not cover the cost of laying the tracks. Then a pouring rain came and washed them out and derailed the engine.

The disappointed engineer tore down the fence, closed the show, and turned to some other idea he had in mind. After all, working out an idea was far more exciting than trying to sell it to the public!

This was just four years since Richard Trevithick had built his first locomotive for the owner of the iron foundry in Wales. From Wales he had gone up to Newcastle, the big coal-mining center on the River Tyne.

There he had built his second locomotive. This one had been ordered by the owner of a colliery (or coal mine) at Wylam, near Newcastle. It was supposed to run on a wooden wagon way, along which horses then pulled coal from the mine to a wharf on the Tyne, where the coal was loaded on boats and shipped down to London.

The owner of the coal mine took one look at the engine when it was finished and refused to accept it. It was too heavy, he said. It would smash the wooden rails into kindling wood. As it would cost too much to lay iron rails, he would keep on using his horses.

All the coal mines along the Tyne used engines for pumping and hoisting, which meant that many engineers and mechanics were needed to look after them. All of these men were interested in Trevithick's engine, especially since it was so much more powerful than that of James Watt, and yet small enough to be put on wheels. One of the most interested was Hedley, the head mechanic at Wylam, who was disappointed that his employer would not put up the money to lay new rails. Another interested mechanic was a brakeman who worked at the Killingworth colliery just across the river from Newcastle. His name was George Stephenson.

During their off-hours a group of men were often to be seen standing about in one of the dingy candlelit taverns, discussing and arguing about the uses to be made of the engine. Sometimes they gathered around the fireplace in George Stephenson's one-room cottage near the Killingworth mine.

Occasionally Richard Trevithick, himself, was there, his fertile brain filled with marvelous ideas for putting his engine to work. Why not use it on the farms? Hitch it to a plow? Or build a threshing machine? Or make a steamboat, which regardless of wind or tide could tow a fire ship into the midst of Napoleon's barges at Boulogne and completely destroy them?

Listening or talking, the big man from Cornwall could not have failed to notice how quick Stephenson was to grasp mechanical principles and problems. It was uncanny, for he had no education at all, and could not even read or write until he was over eighteen. He was then twenty-four, ten years younger than Trevithick.

Work in a coal mine was all that George Stephenson had ever known. As a small boy he began by picking waste pieces out of the coal. Next he drove an engine horse. Then he got work helping his father, who was a fireman. Finally he was put in charge of a pumping engine. By the time he moved to Killingworth to take the job of brakeman, he was married and had a small son named Robert.

Bobby was about two years old when Trevithick first saw him, took him on his knee, and gave him a pony ride on his big boot. The small boy was no more than five when the Cornish giant bade farewell to his friends in Newcastle and set out for London, happy at the prospect of making a great success with his third locomotive—the *Catch Me Who Can*.

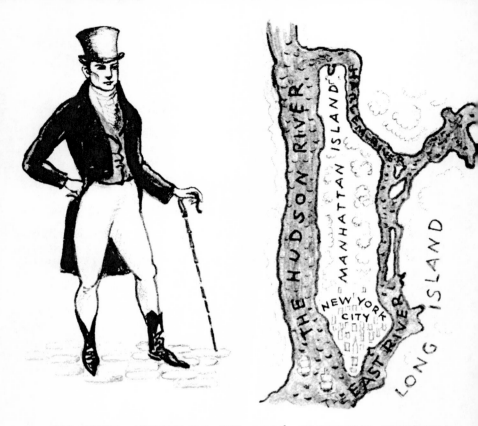

IN THE AUTUMN OF 1806, ROBERT FULTON had returned from France and was in New York City starting to build his steamboat to be used on the Hudson River. Its engine had been shipped from England and would be stored in a warehouse until the hull was finished. This was being built in a shipyard on the East River.

Each day Fulton was there to direct and help with the work. Each morning as he came striding in, swinging

his rattan walking stick, he looked to the workmen like a handsome English lord. Older and more distinguished-looking was his partner, Mr. Robert Livingston, who made frequent visits to see how the steamboat was taking shape. It was to be twice the size of the one they had tried out in Paris—150 feet long and 13 feet wide.

It was to be called *The Clermont,* which was the name of Mr. Livingston's country estate on the Hudson River. By April, the hull was finished and Fulton had it carted across the city to a wharf on the Hudson, where he then installed the engine. Onlookers who hung around to watch the "crazy contraption" being assembled called it "Fulton's Folly" and declared it would never work. But one day, to their amazement, they saw it push off.

On August 9, 1807, exactly four years to the day after he had tried out his steamboat on the Seine, Robert Fulton tested his new *Clermont* on the Hudson and was much pleased with her performance.

"She went three miles an hour," he said, "and beat all sailboats that were trying to stem the tide."

On Monday, August 17, 1807, at one o'clock in the afternoon, *The Clermont* was to make her first voyage up the Hudson from New York to Albany. On deck well before starting time, a fashionable group of people had assembled, members of the Livingston family and their guests. The men were all in elegant ruffled shirts and high hats, the ladies in beribboned bonnets and long, slim skirts.

All were rather silent, wondering if they had been foolish to accept the invitation. Smoke was pouring from the tall chimney in the middle of the boat. Bits of soot

74

came fluttering down upon them. Soon a signal was given, the ropes untied, and the boat began to move.

"Then," said Fulton, describing the next dreadful moment, "the boat moved a short distance and then stopped and became immovable. I could distinctly hear [people mutter], 'I told you it was so. It is a foolish scheme. I wish I were well out of it.'

"I elevated myself upon a platform and addressed the assembly. I stated that I knew not what was the matter, but if they would be quiet and indulge me for half an hour, I would either go on or abandon the voyage for that time. I went below and examined the machinery and discovered a slight maladjustment. In a short time the boat was again in motion. She continued to move."

Little by little, as the paddle wheels continued to splash and creak and the boat kept steadily moving ahead, the passengers became relaxed. And as they were passing through the highlands, they began singing a Scottish ballad, "Ye Banks and Braes of Bonny Doon."

In late afternoon everyone was quite ready to enjoy a delicious supper of roast chicken, ham, gingerbread, green apple tarts, spice cake, and early purple plums that had been gathered in Mr. Livingston's orchard.

From the time it started, the steamboat had been causing amazement and alarm on the river. Fishermen, as they saw it coming, pulled in their nets in frantic haste and rowed for the shore. Captains on some of the larger sailing boats shook their fists at it and hoped it would break down. They saw it as a rival threatening their livelihood. In the dark of night, it was even more terrifying. Each load of pine logs thrown into the boiler sent up a flaming cloud of smoke and sparks.

On board, the ladies spent that first night on cots in the cabin, while the gentlemen stretched out on the deck until sunrise. Tuesday was a beautiful day and an especially happy one for Robert Fulton. At about one o'clock, as they were nearing Clermont, Mr. Livingston's estate, that gentleman strode to the bow of the boat and called for silence. He then announced the engagement of his niece, Harriet Livingston, to his esteemed partner, Robert Fulton, whose name he prophesied would go down in history as a "benefactor of the world." He also predicted that before the end of the century, steamboats might well be traveling to Europe.

The party spent Tuesday night at Clermont, leaving the next morning at nine for Albany, which was forty miles farther on. Friday afternoon they were back in New York after a most successful trip. Fulton figured that his steamboat had gone 150 miles in thirty-two hours, while one of the river sloops took an average of four days to sail from New York to Albany.

"The power of propelling boats by steam is now fully proved," he wrote a friend. "However, I will not admit that it is half so important as the torpedo."

Fulton was disappointed in not being able to interest the United States government in his torpedo. Even though he had blown up a ship in New York harbor to prove what it would do, neither Congress nor President Jefferson favored using torpedoes.

In the spring of 1808, *The Clermont,* renamed *The North River,* began making regular trips from New York to Albany and back. The next spring, Fulton wrote his old teacher, Benjamin West, that in one year *The North River* had made a profit of $16,000 and that he was building two more steamboats. So at last, the steamboat gave Robert Fulton his long-coveted fame and fortune.

JAMES MADISON DOLLEY

1809

ON MARCH 4, 1809, JAMES MADISON became president of the United States and, with his very pretty wife, Dolley, moved into the President's House in Washington, D.C. That same year Napoleon divorced Josephine because she had given him no son, and the next year he married young Marie Louise, daughter of the emperor of

Marie Loui

Austria. This meant that Austria was utterly beaten and humbled. England, however, still remained to be conquered.

Thomas Jefferson was not sorry that his eight years as president were over. The last three had been made miserable by Napoleon's new kind of war against England.

After the destruction of the French fleet at Trafalgar, Napoleon talked no more about invading England. Instead he struck at her shipping trade, hoping to defeat her by starvation. No ship, he decreed, carrying goods from England would be allowed to enter any port in France, or that of any country under his control.

England's reply to this was a decree that any ship of any nation carrying goods to any port in Napoleon's empire would be seized by the British as a prize of war.

Up to this time, American ships had been very active in the prosperous business of carrying wheat, cotton, fish, and other supplies to Europe. Suddenly, ship after ship was seized by England. And not only ships but also American sailors. England had always claimed the right to search American ships to find deserters from her navy. During the long war against Napoleon, so many thousands had deserted that United States sailors were also being seized and forced into the British service.

This outrage brought a cry for "War against England." To avoid getting into war, President Jefferson proposed, and Congress approved, an embargo. This was an act designed to keep American ships out of trouble by forbidding them to leave their home ports. It was hoped that cutting off their supplies from America might bring the British and the French to terms. Unfortunately it had no effect on either of them, while it was ruining American shipowners. So on his last sad day in office, Thomas Jefferson signed a repeal of the embargo.

Now President James Madison and his Congress had to deal with the awful problem. First they passed an act allowing American ships to trade with any nation except France or England. And trade would be resumed with whichever one of them was first to repeal its laws against American shipping.

Napoleon pretended to do this, and so tricked the United States into turning against England. On June 18, Congress declared war against England, which came to be known as the War of 1812.

from an English cartoon

IN THE SUMMER OF 1812 NAPOLEON was in Russia. He had gone there to punish the tsar, who had refused to keep his harbors closed to the English.

The tsar needed the English market for his wheat and lumber and did not propose to take orders from that self-made French emperor. Instead the tsar prepared to teach that creature a lesson he would not soon forget!

In June, with a splendid army of 600,000 men, Napoleon was marching toward Moscow. Ahead of him the tsar's army kept retreating, destroying the countryside and leaving the French army with nothing to live on. When the French finally reached Moscow, they found the city deserted. It had also been set on fire, and as the fire spread, the whole city went up in flames.

Winter came before Napoleon could swallow his pride

enough to give up and go home. Then his ragged troops, dressed for summer, blinded by freezing blizzards, died by thousands along the way. Some were even frozen to death sitting upright on their horses. Hardly more than half of Napoleon's once-great army lived to reach France. His journey to Russia to punish the tsar had been such a disaster that it gave the nations of Europe new hope.

England, Russia, Prussia, Spain, and Sweden joined against him. Then, at last, his army ruined, surrounded by a ring of enemies, betrayed and deserted by his own officers, the world's most famous man, "destroyer of the peace of Europe," finally fell.

On April 14, 1814, Napoleon signed his abdication and was taken away to the island of Elba.

1814

NAPOLEON'S DEFEAT LEFT ENGLAND FREE to pay more attention to war against the United States. Troops no longer needed in Europe were sent to America. An attack on Washington, D.C., came first. One August day a post rider dashed into the city with news that the British fleet was in Chesapeake Bay.

President Madison was not there when a messenger arrived at the President's House telling Mrs. Madison to leave at once. It was not a moment too soon. As four galloping horses drew her coach out of town by one road, the enemy soldiers, entering by another, made straight for the President's House. Finding the long table set for dinner, they piled up the chairs, put a live coal to the pile, and so set the house on fire. The fire spread through the town. Next day a hurricane added to the damage the fire had done, but when the storm of two days was over, the British soldiers had left.

President and Mrs. Madison were able to return. They found the outer walls of the President's House still standing, but so streaked with smoke and water, it seemed best to paint the house white. So it began to be called the "White House." In 1902, President Theodore Roosevelt made "White House" the official name.

From Washington, the British fleet sailed north up Chesapeake Bay to Baltimore, which was protected by a fort. All the night of September 13, 1814, guns from the British battleships bombarded the fort. All night, from one of those British ships, a young American lawyer, Francis Scott Key, who had gone aboard to see about releasing a prisoner, listened to the booming of the cannon. At daybreak, he was so thrilled to see the stars and stripes still flying above the fort that, on the back of an old letter, he began to write the now-famous words of

THE STAR-SPANGLED BANNER.

The next night in Baltimore it was sung for the first time to the tune of an old English ditty. For over one hundred years people continued to sing it. In 1931, it was declared the United States national anthem.

The crown of the Austrian Empire

AFTER NAPOLEON HAD BEEN BANISHED to the island of Elba, came the "glorious moment" for the kings and emperors to put the continent of Europe back again the way they wanted it. They met in Vienna, invited by the Austrian emperor, Francis II. Emperors, kings, archdukes, and princes came riding in, each one escorted by a retinue of diplomats and advisors and attended by mounted guards, bands of musicians, and servants of all kinds. Never again would there be such a dazzling display of gold braid, waving plumes, and sparkling jewels as was seen at that Congress of Vienna.

Ludwig van Beethoven was also there, invited by the emperor to entertain his royal guests. Since 1809, when his Fifth Symphony was published, Beethoven's fame had been steadily growing. And today, when the names of those attending the Congress are all but forgotten, the name of the great musician lives on. His *Fidelio* was the first opera performed for the visitors. They also heard the famous *Eroica,* as well as a cantata, especially composed for the occasion, entitled "The Glorious Moment."

It was not long before the moments of the Congress became anything but glorious. Polite discussion turned into nasty arguments and then into downright squabbling. Austria and England were actually talking about going to war against Prussia and Russia, when suddenly the bickering was cut short by the awful news that Napoleon had escaped from Elba and was back again in France!

Once again, kings and emperors were united by their common enemy. Once again their armies marched against him. It was about one hundred days from Napoleon's escape from Elba to his final defeat by Wellington, the English commander, at the village of Waterloo.

Napoleon was then sent to Saint Helena, a rocky island in the south Atlantic, where he was kept a prisoner for six years, until his death in 1821. Looking back on his defeat, Napoleon could not admit that anyone but himself had been responsible for it.

"I, myself," he said, "have been the cause of my own disastrous fate: I have been my own worst enemy."

THE LONG WAR AGAINST NAPOLEON, which had brought so many unexpected results, also brought the day of the railroad. During the war, the cost of food for horses rose so enormously high that mine owners began to think it would be cheaper to use a steam engine that needed nothing but fuel and water, even though it meant replacing the wooden rails.

The change-over began at the coal mines near Newcastle. The Wylam wagon way, which had been much too fragile for Richard Trevithick's engine, was replaced with iron rails, and Hedley, the head mechanic at Wylam, built the first engine for it. Another engineer paid thirty pounds for the use of Trevithick's patent and built a locomotive to be used at a coal mine near Leeds.

x-the flange

George Stephenson, who saw both of these new engines tried out, was also given his chance. Since Trevithick had been there, Stephenson had risen from brakeman at the Killingworth colliery to head engineer. In 1813, toward the end of the year, one of the owners of the mine ordered him to supervise the building of a locomotive in the colliery workshops. On July 25, 1814, the locomotive was ready to be tried out. A throng of miners and their families watched as it ran slowly but steadily past the Stephenson cottage on the moor.

The wheels of this engine had flanges on the inside to keep them from slipping off the rails. Otherwise, it was

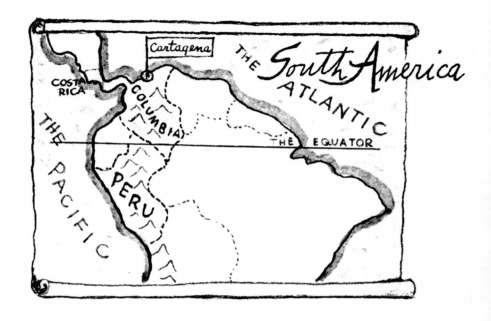

no different from the locomotive built ten years too soon by the Cornish giant, Richard Trevithick.

Where was Richard Trevithick on that day? And what was he thinking about? Not about a locomotive.

He was now excited about the pumping engines he was going to install in the silver mines in Peru. He had just signed the agreement. Soon he would sail for South America to share in the enormous profits to be made from the silver. It would be many years before he was back again in England.

By that time, not he, but George Stephenson was beginning to be called the "Father of the Locomotive."

The success of his first locomotive had brought Stephenson's name to the notice of influential men in and around Newcastle. One of these was a wool merchant and banker at Darlington. He was interested in promoting a railway to run from there to Stockton ten miles away on the Tees River. It was to be a public railway—the first public railway ever to be built.

In 1821, George Stephenson was asked to lay out the right of way. His son Robert had by then finished school and went with his father as assistant surveyor. Next, they formed a company to build the engines, with Robert as business manager and his father in charge of the factory. Their first engine was called simply *Locomotion*.

The promoters of the Darlington Stockton Railroad made the opening day of this first public railroad one to be long remembered. They distributed 300 tickets to the

stockholders, but another three hundred people had crowded on by the time *Locomotion* took off on its first run from Darlington to Stockton. It was preceded by a man on horseback, followed by ten coal cars, twenty-four carriages full of people, and twenty-four more horsedrawn carriages for the less fortunate who failed to get on the train. It ran about eight miles an hour. A crowd of forty thousand screaming, cheering people greeted its arrival in Stockton. Seven cannon thundered a salute. Bands struck up "God Save the King." Church bells rang. A banquet was held in the town hall to honor the inventor, George Stephenson.

Robert Stephenson did not attend the banquet. He was not in England. He was in South America, having expected to make a fortune installing engines in the gold and silver mines being reopened in the mountains of

Colombia. But the mountains were so high and the trails so steep and narrow, there was no way to get the engines up to the mines. So he was much relieved when the time came for him to return to England. It was spring of 1827.

He was at an inn in the seaport of Cartagena, waiting for his ship, when among all the Spanish being spoken, he happened to hear two men speaking English. One of them especially caught his attention—a tall, gaunt, big-boned man, in shabby clothes and a wide straw hat.

"His name is Trevithick," said the innkeeper.

And so it was. Richard Trevithick! After years of almost unbelievable hardship and danger, he had left Peru, made his way to Costa Rica and from there to Cartagena. He stared incredulously at the young stranger who introduced himself as Robert Stephenson.

"Bobby? Can you be Bobby?" He turned to his companion, "Many's the time I've dandled this young fellow on my knee."

Trevithick was destitute. Robert gave him enough to pay his passage back to England. There he died six years later, penniless, but as always filled with hope and imagination—a giant still in mind and spirit.

INDEX

CPSIA information can be obtained at www.ICGtesting.com
Printed in the USA
BVOW02s2011220916

462879BV00002B/2/P